MW00339251

MILITARY STYLE INVADES FASHION

MILITARY
STYLE
INVADES
FASHION

TIMOTHY GODBOLD

WITH AN INTRODUCTION BY
COLIN MCDOWELL

PREFACE

Once you begin to notice the extent to which military styles have influenced fashion, it's impossible to ignore it. Militaria is unmistakable and it is everywhere: worn by men, women and children across the globe.

From high fashion to thrift-store chic, military appropriations are ubiquitous. Luxury fashion houses have long borrowed elements of both ceremonial swagger and utilitarianism from the style sheet of military uniform. In the 1960s, Yves Saint Laurent designed his famous pea coats, igniting a trend for exquisite military-inspired clothing and coats soon followed by designers including Dries Van Noten, Balmain and Givenchy, among many others. Accessories have also benefitted from similar inspiration, evidenced by Tom Ford's aviator sunglasses and Louis Vuitton handbags and luggage. At the other end of the fashion scale, in the 1960s, hippies wore cargo pants and army jackets as political statements. Now camouflage prints are visible on anything from Nike athletic shoes to bandages and sticking plasters for children. The military influence even goes beyond clothes to interior design, seen in campaign chairs with leather straps and austere lines, to portable Hermes desks.

My interest in the influence of military style on fashion began when I was young. I grew up in Australia in an English family that had emigrated just before the outbreak of World War II. War, and the stories of war, were a significant part of my family's history.

My great grandfather, Alexander Niven, returning home after a holiday in Scotland before World War I, was pulled over on the road and forced to enlist into the ambulance division as he was one of the few who knew how to drive at the time. My grandfather, Harry Godbold, served in the Australian Army in North Africa in World War II. A member of the intelligence division, he was one of 'The Rats of Tobruk' besieged in the Libyan port. And my father, David Godbold, completed his military training while he studied architecture in Melbourne. The war may have been behind us, but we continued to live it in our living room every Saturday afternoon in the stories told and retold.

I remember my father's wardrobe in the spare room at home, where his army uniform hung neatly next to his crested blazer from Trinity College, Melbourne. This wardrobe was a constant fascination to me growing up for the way in which its contents represented power, intellect and sophistication. I noticed the nuances of clothing and how what we wear affects how we feel and behave. I also noticed how costumes functioned in movies – how often, for example, the villains' frightening outfits were derived from extreme military looks, such as those of the SS or the Gestapo. I saw how rock musicians, from the Beatles to Duran Duran and beyond, referenced military clothing in their stage costumes and on their album covers.

I once came across a photograph of Lord Albert Victor in full military regalia. The striking blue and the encrusted gold and silver used in the trimmings and sashes were strong and imperial. They were powerful evidence of the genius that underlay military design. Then I caught sight of myself in a mirror. Following men's fashion that year, I was dressed in fatigue cargo pants tucked into leather boots and a loden green sweater. My hair was slicked back as severely as if I had just stepped out of a plane after flying a bombing mission in World War II. I laughed at myself, of course, but the echoes between the photograph and my own clothes made me determined to explore further. Where does our fascination with military style come from and how far will we take it in the name of fashion?

This book looks at types of military style and how they have been absorbed into the mainstream of fashion. Each chapter reveals a different visual aspect of the military style vocabulary, celebrating its widespread appeal. In other words why, as the cultural critic Troy Patterson observed recently in *The New York Times*, 'half the people you see on the street are dressed to kill.'

THE FASHION INVASION
COLIN MCDOWELL

It might seem that there is a clear contradiction at the heart of military clothing when co-opted into the world of fashion. While fashion appears to be concerned, above all else, with self-expression, freedom, and individuality, military dress tends to be about anonymity, the subordination of the self to the group, and adherence to often random rules.

In fact, the two worlds are closer than might be expected. The world of fashion is based on strict sartorial rules about what goes with what and what should be worn when, while its followers have their own hierarchy in which designer logos, the cut of a suit or the height of a heel indicate the wearer's bona fides within the vast band of wannabes. For their part, armies around the world have long understood the importance of an impressive sartorial presence, both in its officers in order to inspire a subtle mixture of loyalty and fear in their men, and in the men themselves in order to build *esprit de corps* through uniformity. The military holds its members to impeccable dress standards, even amid the privations and dangers of a combat zone. In terms of dress code, any officers' mess around the world is as demanding to get into as the newest and most 'happening' of nightclubs – and only the most dedicated dandy can legitimately pay as much attention to his appearance as a member of the military elite does, not only for 'a full dress' night, but also for the daily duty parade.

The military look is purloined or re-created at all levels of fashion, from the couture catwalk to the generic fashion retailers of the 1990s and 2000s and the social outcasts and rebels in between. The focus of this book is on the twenty-first century, showing that the military influence remains as strong as ever. Even as the world wars recede into history and conflict has instead become closely associated with the deserts of Afghanistan and the Middle East, fashion designers and thrift-store scavengers find elements of dress that appeal across the board with their echoes of bravery and courage, authority, menace or the glamour of fear. Echoes of militarism still have the power to provoke. When Beyoncé dressed her dancers in black leather for the Superbowl halftime in 2016, she caused controversy because the costumes were seen by some to echo the military look co-opted by the Black Panthers, the controversial political party of the late 1960s. Whether or not it was subconscious or unconscious, it made the point that uniform is not merely about the military. It crosses into many seemingly unlikely areas that affect us all, and they in turn are all political.

In many ways, the influence of military dress on modern fashion continues a process that can be traced back even before the emergence of distinct military uniforms in France in the mid-seventeenth century. In the late fifteenth and sixteenth centuries, German mercenary soldiers known as Landsknecht fought in wars throughout Europe. Their founder, the Holy Roman Emperor Maximilian I, excused them from the sumptuary laws that regulated the clothes worn by normal citizens, and the Landsknecht were distinguished by their slashed doublets, through which they pulled folds and puffs of their shirts, and their multicoloured hose. Far removed from its army-camp origins, slashing soon became a common element of European noble dress, once courts and couriers had legitimized what had once been seen as barbaric and fearsome by turning dress meant to terrify into a fashion statement meant to beguile, often with a degree of fashion camp far from the original.

The Highlanders at Waterloo, 1815, Felix Phillippoteaux

While most earlier armies had comprised either hired mercenaries or hastily conscripted farmers and peasants who had to return to the fields during the harvest season, the seventeenth century saw the rise of professional national armies. Where previous soldiers had distinguished themselves from the enemy by wearing coloured sashes, new armies wore generally standardized uniforms. The French introduced the regimental system, based on the idea that it was easier to build loyalty among a small group of comrades than to an amorphous and anonymous army. These small units were distinguished by potent, variations to collars, cuffs and coloured facings. This was the start of the evolution of the complex symbolism of military uniform that still prevails to a degree today.

The predominant colours were deep blues and madders – the famous scarlet of the British redcoats was more expensive to dye, so most armies avoided it – which helped soldiers to see and be seen on battlefields covered with clouds of smoke from gunpowder weapons. Precision of appearance was highly prized. At a time when battles were fought in formations of precise military ranks, the appearance of a well-drilled body of soldiers moving together in identical, perfect uniforms helped to strike fear into the heart of the enemy. Such was the glamour and exhibitionism

British soldiers in the 19th Hussars cavalry, c.1860

associated with such clothing that it attracted the attention of the British fashion leader Prince George, the Prince Regent, and later King George IV. The prince was fascinated by warfare – although not enough to risk becoming personally involved in any military action – and diverted himself by designing showy uniforms for his armies. They were, alas, indistinguishable from the uniforms of the enemy, Napoleon's Grande Armée. There is a story that, later, George IV enjoyed recounting his heroic deeds in the eventual defeat of Napoleon at Waterloo in 1815 – a battle at which he was not actually present – to the Duke of Wellington, the victorious general in the battle and another leader of British society fashion who, we can assume, remained silent throughout.

Soldiers for much of the nineteenth century were still the soldiers with which we are familiar from the novels of Jane Austen: grenadiers and hussars, with bright costumes, large bearskin hats and glinting buttons. Their glamour disguised the horror of battlefields that the vast majority of the population never saw. It was only with the advent of photography during conflicts such as the American Civil War (1861–65) that most people came face-to-face with the brutal reality of warfare. By then, however, the glamour of soldiering was well established as a theme in popular culture, encouraging the belief that going into battle would 'make a man of you', which was finally exposed as spurious during World War II, if not earlier.

Uniform changed, as new rapid-firing and smokeless weapons such as the machine gun made it dangerous to wear bright clothes on the battlefield.

Belgian troops early in World War I (1914–18) were described as being 'as conspicuous as claret stains on a new tablecloth.' Those countries who sent troops wearing bright scarlet into the trenches soon decided that discretion was the better part of valour and adopted the drab shades of blue, green and grey that came to dominate the military wardrobe during the twentieth century. The exhibitionist glamour of the parade ground was joined in the public psyche by an acknowledgement of the dangers and privations of military action – themselves linked with manliness and therefore believed to be glamorous.

Not that military peacockery was abandoned altogether. Uniform became divided into two distinct types. One was uniform for action, which was more practical, less bright, and more easily maintained. It is echoed today in the extensive use of khakis and camouflage in civilian clothing of which more later, alongside this field dress, formal dress uniform was retained for ceremonial use, ensuring that at least on public occasions (battle is a very private, enclosed affair), modern members of the military are as disciplined and self-controlled when it comes to their appearance as their forebears.

In a world that was still in the shadow of World War I, when millions of men were conscripted, no civilians would have dreamed of wearing military clothing in normal life, although Coco Chanel – one of fashion's great iconoclasts – was so enamoured with the clothes of her lovers that she added military-style pockets to women's jackets. After the rise of extremist politics in the 1920s, Mussolini's fascists in Italy and Hitler's Nazis in Germany deliberately adopted clothing that resembled uniform – paramilitary clothing – in order to give their followers the appearance and credentials of a military organization. The same tactic was adopted later by Che Guevara and Fidel Castro, who adopted military fatigues in their revolutionary campaign in Cuba in the 1950s. Meanwhile Mao Zedong, who led China's communists to power in 1949, dressed the entire Chinese population in an equivalent of military uniform based on baggy, virtually identical fatigues: a visual symbol of the loss of individuality he believed necessary in a Maoist society.

Chinese military uniform, 1966

If the military silhouette and military styling have been intermittently popular since at least the Landsknecht of the sixteenth century, wearing military dress itself only became fashionable far more recently, in the aftermath of World War II. Not only did governments suddenly want to sell off huge amounts of military surplus clothing to recoup some money; war movies also enhanced the appeal of military clothing by dressing matinee idols in uniform for the big screen so that even the least pugnacious civilian could have his John Wayne moment, on the safe streets of major cities.

It was the 1960s, however, that saw young people deliberately co-opt military dress as a way to express their rejection of the established order that such clothes represented, inspired in part by the examples of Che Guevara and Castro. Many protestors against the Vietnam War, including veterans of that conflict, made a point of wearing ripped and patched army fatigues. Militaria had become a symbol of rebellion and revolution – or was it pre-eminently largely a disguise for young men not as sure of their masculinity or 'street cred' as they would like to be seen and use uniform to deflect possible critical comment.

Versace, Spring/Summer 2016, Milan

A zebra could be said to be a horse wishing to draw attention to itself – and that is a fair description of many fashionistas who wear camouflage today. Truly fashionable people – in no way the same creatures as a fashionista – do not wear camouflage. Or, at least, camouflage that looks like camouflage. They wear something quite other, something that has had even a smidgen of creative thinking to it. Look how Andy Warhol made camouflage patterns and shapes into something very new, exciting and with its own creative probity merely by changing the colours from military khaki to Pantone primaries. Not everyone wishes to wallow in the mud: the 'take-up' on his idea, like the take-up of most of his ideas, has been phenomenal, and universal. And it has had its postmodern-way moment, too. By necessity, military camouflage must be tough, durable and disguising.

Fashion plays no part whatsoever in its design or its practicality. But fashion is hard to exclude from any good idea so we have Louis Vuitton bags and travel bags in camouflage. In 2016 Donatella Versace produced a collection almost entirely made of camouflage print, including evening wear. Even earlier, Jean Paul Gaultier – one of the fashion world's great masters of legerdemain – gave it couture status in many of his collections. Street meets style? Some might say so. Or is it style goes popularist?

But military is not just about the twentieth century and even more recent purloining by high fashion of basic camouflage. When Bathsheba Everdene had her fatal meeting with Sergeant Troy, it wasn't just his dazzling, phallic sword-play in the film version of Thomas Hardy's elegiac novel, *Far From the Madding Crowd*, it was also his tightly fitted, perfectly cut scarlet jacket complete with gilt trimmings that played a considerable part in one of the most famous seductions without touch in any film or literature. And anyone who has read the novels from Jane Austen knows how devastating full military uniform can be to the sensibilities of young women who have lived a sheltered life and, in fact, read too many romantic novels, from *Pride and Prejudice* to *Fifty Shades of Grey*, the perfect romantic novel for our time.

But, it is military dress for war that has the most power over us, and has done so for the last fifty years. Since the Limbo label in Greenwich Village or, 20 years later, Unique on Broadway, opened they have been packed every weekend with kids of every shape, size and ethnicity. Camouflage has frequently sent out a siren cry to high fashion labels such as Tom Ford's Gucci that it has almost earned the right to be considered a classic fashion perennial. The pictures in this book make clear why that is.

CEREMONY

Ceremonial military clothing recalls an age of glamour and allure, with scarlet jackets, towering plumes and glinting sword belts. The grandeur of the parade ground and splendour of the trooping of the colour, for example, has provided much romantic inspiration to the field of fashion, allowing designers to evoke tales of heroism and chivalry.

What is symbolic today had its roots in practicality. The colourful, exaggerated appearance of today's ceremonial dress was originally intended to be worn in the field to impress and terrify the foe, as well as to to bolster the morale of the wearer by making him (inevitably, the warrior was a man) feel stronger and more powerful – part of an unvanquishable whole.

Braiding, for example, enjoys popular use on the front and shoulders of tailored jackets today. However, the original purpose of the iconic gold gilt braiding of old tunics – known as 'frogging' – was to give the chest and shoulders additional protection from the swipe of a sword blade. As it appeared on fur-lined hussar jackets, first worn by cavalry soldiers in the Black Army led by the Hungarian King Matthias Corvinus in the early fifteenth century, it had evolved its own symbolism: the frogging echoed the shape of the ribs, turning the soldiers into living skeletons in order to intimidate the enemy. Furthermore, in the sixteenth century, the winged hussars of Poland added 'wings' of feathers rising from their backs on a wooden frame, supposedly to make a loud noise that scared enemy mounts. Similarly, now merely for ceremonial use, the plume of horsehair atop a soldier's helmet protected the neck from blows.

Small spherical metal buttons could, *in extremis*, be pulled from a soldier's coat and fired from muskets. (It was said that in eighteenth century Prussia, Frederick the Great added additional buttons to cuffs to discourage foot soldiers from wiping their noses on their sleeves.)

The flamboyance of ceremonial military dress has particularly appealed to performers since the 1960s. The Beatles adopted hussar jackets for Sgt Pepper. In 1971 Jimi Hendrix – who enlisted as a paratrooper in the 101st Airborne in 1961 – purchased an antique hussar jacket, which dated back to the mid-1800s. The baton passed to Adam Ant in the early 1980s, who bought actor David Hemming's jacket from the movie *Charge of the Light Brigade* for his 'dandy highwayman' character. The New Romantics put military uniform at the heart of London's club scene. Nick Rhodes of Duran Duran remembered that the band's clothes were part of a premeditated attack: 'Uniforms unified us, projecting the look of solidarity as if we were all part of the same team and looking good, together.' Later in the 1980s, Michael Jackson assumed clothes fit for his status as the King of Pop and had Savile Row tailors Gieves and Hawkes make military jackets for his BAD tour based on the court dress of a British privy counsellor.

The innovations and adaptations of formal military dress into contemporary fashion are endless and creative. For his Spring 2016 women's collection for Givenchy, designer Riccardo Tisci paired officer's coats and jackets not with dresses or skirts as one might expect, but with shorts and knee-high boots with *trompe l'oeil* patterns. His Spring 2016 men's collection featured officer-style buttons and studdings. So influential is Tisci now, that he kicked off another wave of fashionistas finding vintage Hussar jackets and brass button items to wear.

At Balmain, designer Olivier Rousteing filled the Fall 2016 men's collection with looks straight from the officers' mess – double-breasted coats with gleaming buttons, leather cavalry boots and richly embellished braiding-covered jackets.

Gone are the hussars of old, but frogging, outsize buttons and military timepieces have all trickled down into the mainstream. The rich styling of hussar jackets – with their tailored cuts and glints of gilding – and the opulence of ceremonial dress abound in fashion today, bringing the formality and sense of occasion from the world of officers to everyday and evening wear.

Overleaf: Trooping the Colour, London

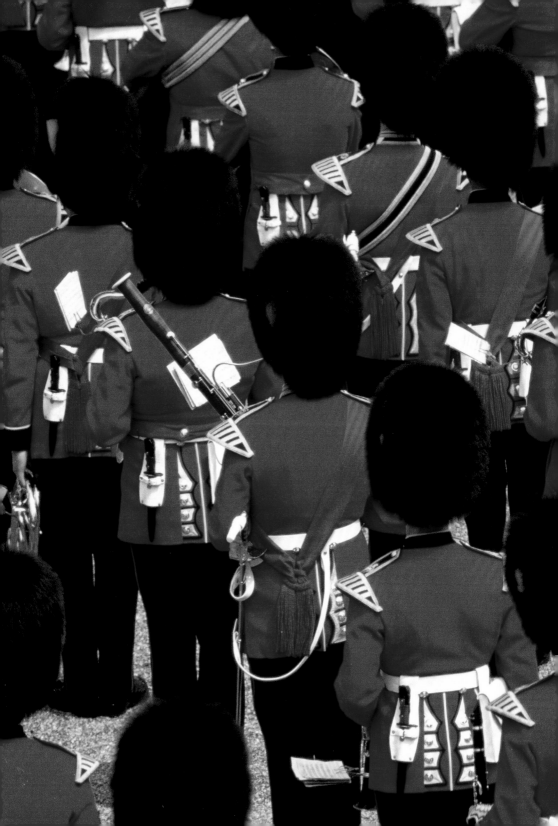

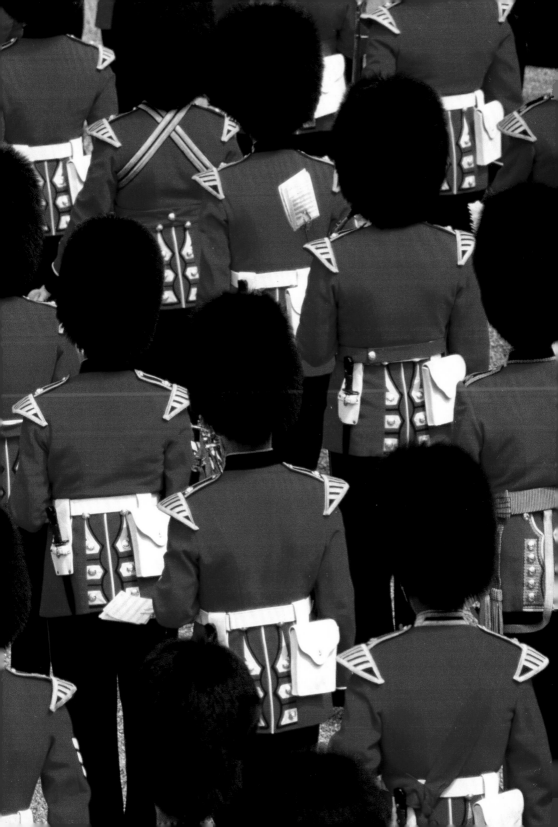

Lieutenant Andrew Finucane, 1811, James Northcote

Balmain, Fall/Winter 2016–17, Paris

Balmain, Fall/Winter 2016–17, Paris

Jean Paul Gaultier, Fall/Winter 2015–16, Paris

Alexander McQueen, Fall/Winter 2016, London

Balmain, Spring/Summer 2009, Paris

Paris, 2015

2013

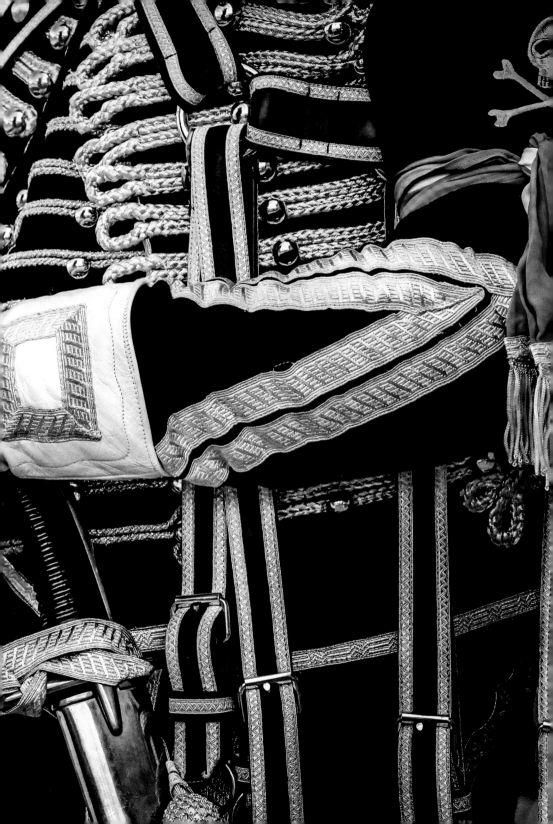

Fashionisto, January 2013

Paris, 2013

Dries Van Noten, Fall/Winter 2016–17, Paris

Vogue, France, August 2010

'TO SEE THE

FORWARD

MARCH OF

MILITARY STYLE

ON DESIGNER RUNWAYS

IS UNSETTLING

ESPECIALLY DURING PERIODS

OF WAR'

———

SUZY MENKES, THE NEW YORK TIMES

Jalouse, France, November 2012

Alfons XIII, King of Spain, 1900s

New York, 2016

CAMPAIGN

For well over a century, fashion has rummaged through the soldier's kitbag. The trench coats, aviator jackets, drab green fatigues, parkas, T-shirts and camouflage regularly available from fashion brands worldwide, are based on uniform fit for military action rather than ceremonial display; designed for practicality rather than exaggeration, for blending in rather than standing out.

The oldest is also the most familiar: the trench coat, as worn by everyone from Humphrey Bogart to Beyoncé. It owed its creation to the English tailor Thomas Burberry, who designed it in 1879 after inventing waterproof gabardine – but it owed its popularity to its adoption by British officers on the Western Front in World War I. With epaulettes to display rank and a chest flap to cover a gun, the coat was light but weatherproof. After the war it was adopted by Hollywood, and began its long association with glamour. Decades later, Burberry offered a trench coat in silk taffeta – and the last place anyone would wear it would be in the rain.

Out of sight – literally – the T-shirt was introduced by the US Navy during the Spanish-American War in 1898. It was intended as an undergarment, however, and was kept hidden by everyone except manual labourers until after World War II, when army surplus filled the bins of thrift stores and the T-shirt became beloved of the young. The glamorous T-shirt arrived in the 1990s, when Helmut Lang added a logo to make the most humble of garments something for the elite to lust after.

The shearling aviator jacket underwent a similar trajectory from practicality to glamour. Designed in World War II to insulate bomber crews flying at high altitudes, the British RAF's Irvin jacket was made from thick sheepskin, with a large collar to protect the neck and a waist belt to stop drafts. The US Army Air Force equivalent, the A-2, combined horse leather with elasticated knit at the waist and cuffs. In the 1980s, appearances in movies such as *Indiana and the Raiders of the Lost Ark* and *Top Gun* made the A-2 a must-have for the Studio 54 set, worn with jeans, obligatory Ray-Ban Wayfarer sunglasses and, for women, high heels. Fast-forward to Burberry in 2010, and Christopher Bailey's versions of British RAF aviator jackets prepared the wearer for a very chic urban battlefield indeed.

The clothes we wear create our own personal mythology, so youth gangs and political movements are particularly drawn to the subversive associations of clothes linked to military discipline and order. In the 1960s, English Mods appropriated the green army parka, while US hippies adopted khaki or camouflage drill jackets and US Navy bell-bottoms to denounce the Vietnam War (it didn't hurt that military surplus was usually cheap). At the end of the twentieth century, camouflage on the streets reflected the dusty, sandy battlefields of Helmand and Fallujah where the War on Terror was being waged.

Since armies first adopted camouflage early in the twentieth century, they have employed artists to develop increasingly effective patterns that work in specific environments, including famous artists such as Ellsworth Kelly, Arshile Gorky and Grant Wood. The latest generations are far removed from the irregular 'jigsaw' splotches of different tones. The Germans and Danes use stippled Flecktarn patterns, while the Americans and Canadians use pixilated 'digital' patterns.

The print broke through to mainstream fashion in the 1990s, when camouflage trousers were ubiquitous and commonly teamed with Timberland boots. Since then, camouflage has become a staple from the hip-hop stage to the couture catwalk: John Galliano designed a sensuous, silk camouflage evening dress for Christian Dior in 2001, Louis Vuitton produced camouflage luggage, the pop star Rihanna wore Christopher Kane camouflage sweat pants, and Instagram star Kim Kardashian wore designer camouflage for everything from formal dresses to leisure wear. Donatella Versace responded to the US Army's issue of new kit by designing her own camouflage for the Versace Spring 2015 military-inspired collection: 'Donatella Versace's army aims to make love, not war', announced Laird Borrelli-Persson writing *Vogue* US's review of the collection, 'There's no mistaking a Versace girl, even one in camouflage'.

The enduring popularity of camouflage reflects a deep appeal that goes beyond its early uses as political statement and subcultural associations. Everyday clothing such as T-shirts, parkas and trench coats have become so integrated into the ordinary fashion vocabulary that they have long lost their ties with their military origins. Designed for practicality, comfort and durability, combat style has proved to be a champion of the off-duty look.

Overleaf: *Vogue*, Japan, June 2015

Tuskegee pilots with fighter airplane, Alabama, 1942

Balmain, Fall/Winter 2014–15, Paris

Burberry Prorsum, Fall/Winter 2010, London

Milan, 2016

'TO WEAR AN

ARMY GREEN JACKET

WHILE REMAINING INNOCENT OF THE CONSEQUENCES OF

DONNING

THE GENUINE ARTICLE ... IS THE

DEFINITION OF LUXURY.'

—

TROY PATTERSON, THE NEW YORK TIMES MAGAZINE

Prabal Gurung, Fall/Winter 2013–14, New York

Milan, 2015

Balmain, Fall/Winter 2014–15, Paris

Medal on the uniform of a US soldier

Yohji Yamamoto, Spring/Summer, 2006, Paris

Milan, 2016

Tokyo, 2016

Rudsak, Spring 2015, Toronto

Seoul, 2015

Versace, Spring/Summer 2016, Milan

'CAMOUFLAGE HAS CAPTURED THE FASHION IMAGINATION.'

—

VANESSA FRIEDMAN, THE NEW YORK TIMES

Versace, Spring/Summer 2016, Milan

Paris, 2014

London, 2014

Maharishi, Spring/Summer 2016, London

Ovadia & Sons, Fall/Winter 2016, New York

New York, 2016

New York, 2015

New York, 2016

Chicago, 2015

New York, 2016

New York, 2014

Burberry Prorsum, Fall/Winter 2010, London

Phoenix, December 2014

London, 2015

Prabal Gurung, Fall 2013, New York

Paris, 2014

Burberry Prorsum, Fall/Winter 2009–10, Milan

LEGIONNAIRE

Since countries in the West began conquering far-flung lands, soldiering has had a strong link with heat and dust: from Napoleon in Egypt, the building of the British Raj in India, to the US Cavalry in the scrublands of the Southwest and Mexico. These campaigns influenced adaptations in uniform to suit the new environs, resulting in lightweight, practical clothing in beige and khaki, made from natural, breathable materials. This practical aesthetic is also accompanied by boy's-own stories of war and derring-do in the world's deserts, which reached a peak in the imagined romance of the French Foreign Legion, introduced to cinema audiences in 1939 by matinee idol Gary Cooper in the action adventure, *Beau Geste*. Legionnaire style in fashion capitalizes on both the practicality and the exoticism evoked by desert and tropical military campaigns.

Founded in 1831 for the French conquest of Algeria, the French Foreign Legion was infamous for its policy of recruiting anyone, no questions asked. Legionnaires came from any nation or any background, escaping from the law, running away from home, hiding from debtors. If they survived the brutal induction, the criminals, rogues, and ne'er-do-wells became men without a past. (The modern Legion remains an elite but less romantic unit – they now carry out background checks on all recruits.) Legionnaires' cylindrical, flat-topped, brimmed white *kepi* is quite recognizable. The Legion clung to parade-ground scarlet trousers, navy blue jackets and heavy greatcoats for marching until the twentieth century when they followed the changes to British army desert uniform.

In the 1840s, soldiers in the Indian Army – British and native soldiers serving under British officers – began to wear drab-coloured clothes to standardize variations in the uniforms of native troops from different regions. Soldiers are said to have used tea, curry powder and mud to dye their clothes the same colour, which became known as *khaki*, from the Urdu word meaning 'dust', and was made the official uniform for the British advance into Abyssinia in 1867.

There are similar stories of sartorial adaptation of uniform to culture and climate through history. Skinner's Horse – a cavalry unit founded by the son of a Scottish father and a Rajput mother – wore long jackets called *kurtas* dyed a rich yellow. The yellow drew on an old Rajput tradition of 'clothes for the dead', signalling that the wearer was prepared to die to achieve victory. The British officer T. E. Lawrence, better known as 'Lawrence of Arabia', adopted the Arabian *dishdasha* (long robes) and *keffiyeh* (head scarf) while helping the Arab Revolt against the Turkish Ottoman Empire during World War I.

Of course, dressing for warm climates is a question not only of style but also of function. British khaki was so effective that it was taken up by military forces around the world in the late nineteenth and early twentieth centuries. The US Army adopted khaki in 1898. Enlisted men integrated their service trousers into everyday use after World War II. Thanks to their comfort, durability and crisp creases, khakis and chinos were adopted by both men and women for warm-weather trousers, skirts and, for more formal wear, suits.

The safari jacket followed a similar trajectory. As its epaulettes, four bellows (pleated) pockets and waist belt suggest, it was originally modelled on a nineteenth-century military jacket. Just before World War II, it was adopted by adventurers heading out on safari in Africa (the US novelist and enthusiastic big-game hunter Ernest Hemingway even designed his own). Recalling his own youth in Algeria, Yves Saint Laurent made the belted silhouette famous with his Safari collection in 1968, and it has since been revisited many times by designers including Ralph Lauren and Bottega Veneta. Although the safari suit may have reached its heyday in the 1970s, safari jackets are mainstays, available from luxury outfitters to mass-market outlets like Gap.

There's more than a hint of the legionnaire style in the modern movement toward sustainable, environmentally friendly fashion, because of the military's history of using natural fabrics and dyes suitable for warm climates. The London designer Christopher Raeburn has reused decommissioned parachutes in his collections. In Los Angeles the designer Greg Lauren deconstructs surplus naval and army items before rebuilding them as tailored military and safari jackets, cargo pants, parkas and other items that he describes as part artist, part nomad, part soldier and part athlete.

Today, you would be hard pressed to find someone who doesn't own a khaki bush jacket, a pair of cargo pants, or an expedition shirt. White and khaki is a fashion match made in heaven for warm weather, from poplin suits in London to cargo shorts on the beaches of Miami. They also signal a preference for practical clothes above frivolous 'fashion'. As explorers setting out to discover the modern world and our place within it, we dress prepared for the journey.

Overleaf: French Foreign Legion, 1950s

Altuzarra, Spring 2013, New York

Ermenegildo Zegna, D&G and Hackett, Spring/Summer 2011

Thierry Mugler, Spring/Summer 2008, Paris

Altuzarra, Spring 2013, New York

'THE WAY THAT PEOPLE
DRESS MAKES THEM
PART OF AN
ARMY,
DRESSED IN THEIR
OWN UNIFORM,
DETERMINED
TO DO
SOMETHING.'

SUZY MENKES, ANOTHER MAGAZINE

Ralph Lauren, Spring 2015, New York

Overleaf: French Foreign Legion uniforms, Biltine, Chad, 1984

Felipe Oliveira Baptista, Spring/Summer 2014, Paris

Salvatore Ferragamo, Spring/Summer 2011, Milan

'ALL MEN ARE EQUAL IN THE FACE OF DUTY, SHARING EQUAL HONOUR, VALOUR AND TRUTH'

—

ALEXANDER MCQUEEN'S SPRING 2015 SHOW NOTES

Canali, Spring/Summer 2016 collection, Milan

Bottega Veneta, Spring/Summer 2016, Milan

Jean Paul Gaultier, 30th Anniversary Show, 2016, Paris

Versace, Spring/Summer 2016, Milan

Victoria Beckham, Spring/Summer 2015, New York

DAZZLE

In the natural world, camouflage is key for survival. It helps animals blend into a background. In military terms, too, camouflage is about disguise and concealment. Remove camouflage from its intended environment, however, and its effect is quite the opposite. When camouflage becomes part of fashion, it calls attention to itself. Nowhere is this more true than in a pattern so bold that you could be forgiven for not realizing it ever had a role as camouflage: dazzle. These stark patterns of geometrical shapes in contrasting colours were never intended to conceal. They were only intended to confuse.

Dazzle was an invention of World War I. Soon after the war began in 1914, the British zoologist John Graham Kerr contacted Winston Churchill, then First Lord of the British Admiralty. Supported by the US artist and camouflage expert Abbot H. Thayer, Kerr suggested that the British use disruptive patterns from the animal kingdom – particularly the zebra, jaguar, and giraffe – to make the boat less conspicuous and harder to locate with a range-finder. In 1917, the idea was furthered by the marine artist and naval officer Norman Wilkinson, who proposed that dazzle should be used to confuse the enemy as to the ship's type size and speed, rather than its position.

The task of painting ships with contrasting blocks of colour fell to the artist Edward Wadsworth, who had to come up with unique patterns for each vessel, so that not even the class of ship it belonged to would be clear. Wadsworth 'dazzled' some 4,000 British merchant ships and 400 Royal Navy vessels, while more than 1,200 US ships were also 'razzle-dazzled'.

The jury is still out on the effectiveness of the technique, but in any case by World War II better range-finders and radar made dazzle largely redundant. The dazzle pattern endured, however. It was a favourite of Pablo Picasso, who saw clear links between dazzle and Cubism. In 1983 a post-World War I painting by Edward Wadsworth himself, *Dazzle-ships in Drydock at Liverpool*, inspired the British graphic designer Peter Saville to use the technique on the cover of *Dazzle Ships*, an album by the electronic band, Orchestral Manoeuvres in the Dark.

In 2004, Hardy Blechman, founder of the fashion label Maharishi, writing with Alex Newman, published *DPM–Disruptive Pattern Material*, a 944-page two-volume encyclopaedic book that charts the history of camouflage, including dazzle, from its inspiration in nature to its interpretation by artists during the Cubist movement, through to its use by anti-war protestors in the 1960s, further exploration by modern artists and into fashion and interior design now. Blechman talks often in interviews about his efforts to rescue camouflage and other disruptive patterns from unhappy associations with war and focus instead on its origins in nature and in art.

On the fashion runway, the aesthetic has been grasped by the menswear designers Simon Spurr in 2012, who credited his inspiration directly to Norman Wilkinson, and Rick Owens in 2013. From disruption to seduction, the hard lines and graphic shapes of dazzle are used to symbolize the self-assured urban male seeking to mark out his individuality in a concrete sea of dullness and beige. In contrast to the orderly stripes on a Breton top, for example, the disrupted lines of dazzle patterns bring a sense of spontaneity and individuality to a garment, which has led to its appeal to both established fashion houses such as Valentino and Christian Dior, as well as young and upcoming labels such as Y3 and Altuzarra. Meanwhile, the disruptive principle itself has become common throughout fashion. Designers set out to confuse the eye to accentuate certain areas of the human body and disguise shortcomings in others. Straight vertical lines make the wearer appear leaner, while distorted lines disrupt a larger area, allowing dazzle to provide an exciting geometry and also flatter the figure.

Overleaf: British gunboat 'HMS Kildangan' in dazzle camouflage, 1918

Valentino, Fall/Winter 2015–16, Paris

Three Society, Fall/Winter 2015–16, Shanghai

New York, 2015

Milan, 2016

Double Standard Clothing, Fall 2015, New York

Simon Spurr, Spring 2012, New York

'MILITARY INFLUENCE

ON FASHION IS

SO PERVASIVE

THAT WE ARE ALMOST

BLIND TO IT'

———

ALICE FISHER, THE GUARDIAN

Madame Figaro, December 2014

Christian Dior, Spring/Summer 1993, Paris

The French Galissonnière class light cruiser, 'Gloire', c.1940

Overleaf: Pink Woman, Spring/Summer 2014

Sydney, 2013

Alibellus +, Spring/Summer 2014, Paris

Y3, Spring/Summer 2016, Paris

Pink Tartan, Spring/Summer 2016, Toronto

'THERE ARE NOW

MORE PEOPLE

ON THE STREET

OUTFITTED

IN WHAT WE THINK OF AS THE

"MILITARY LOOK"

THAN PEOPLE WHO ARE

ACTUALLY IN THE MILITARY.'

—

JULIA REED, THE NEW YORK TIMES

Altuzarra, Spring 2015, New York

Russian Army Design Bureau, Fall/Winter 2015–16, Moscow

Simon Spurr, Spring/Summer 2012, New York

'HMS Tuberose', New York harbour, 1918

Jonathan Saunders, Spring/Summer 2016–17, London

NAUTICAL

The sailor has been a romantic figure for centuries because of his association with the sea – with adventure, mystery and self-reliance. These are the pirates with their huge gauntlet cuffs, admirals in their finery and the bell-bottomed deckhands we know from *On the Town* or *South Pacific*.

As with the soldier, of course, nautical clothes have their origins in the tough life onboard ship. Trousers were wide-bottomed so that they could be rolled up during the frequent washing of the deck or removed quickly if sailors needed to abandon ship; gauntlet cuffs could be folded down to protect the hands while working with ropes; the large buttons of pea coats or the toggles of duffle coats could be fastened by fingers numb with cold. In Britain's Royal Navy, the basic uniform – the Number One rig – still includes a lanyard strung around the neck that was originally used to fire a cannon.

From the fifteenth century, seafaring was central to the rise of European commercial and imperial power, from the Spanish galleons that brought gold from South America to the Dutch trade ships that carried spices from the East Indies and Britain's Royal Navy. In these early fleets, sailors wore what their captains specified, but a widely imitated uniform was made official in Britain in 1857: blue serge frock, flannel trousers, a jumper with a blue 'sailor' collar lined with white tape, a pea jacket, a black handkerchief worn at the neck, and a straw hat to keep off the sun. The US Navy, meanwhile, adopted three styles of uniform: dress, for ceremonial occasions; service for normal wear, often at sea; and workwear – chambray or denim shirts or overalls for hard labour.

In the nineteenth century, the Royal Navy helped Britannia 'rule the waves' and the royal family heightened the glamour of 'nautical chic'. William IV, the 'Sailor King', served in the American Revolution in his youth and 1827 became Lord High Admiral. The connection has endured: more recent naval royals include Kings George V and VI, Lord Mountbatten, Prince Philip, Prince Andrew and Prince William.

William IV's niece, Queen Victoria, is credited with bringing sailor chic onto land, when in 1846 she dressed her four-year-old son Prince Albert Edward in a miniature sailor suit. The look was soon copied in children's nurseries everywhere, and by the 1870s and 1880s was being worn by affluent women in a wide range of colours. Designers such as John Redfern in Cowes on the Isle of Wight adopted the clothes as their clients took to yachting, and the sailor suit has been successfully reinvented for well over a century since, by designers from Coco Chanel at the time of World War I to Mary Quant in the 1960s and Yohji Yamamoto in the twenty-first century.

Working on the coast in Normandy in 1913, Chanel also adopted other aspects of nautical style: the straw boater, wide-bottomed 'beach pyjamas', blue-and-white striped Breton tops, and a knitted jersey variation of the long fisherman's jersey, the *chandail*. Some fifty years later, sailor-inspired clothing, in particular the pea coat, would become an iconic design element in the work of Yves Saint Laurent. The pea coat, in rich wool or cashmere, offered a perfect balance of empowerment, utility and subtle luxury. Generally double-breasted, with large buttons and deep pockets, the pea coat has been a mainstay in young people's wardrobes since Bob Dylan made it part of his signature look in 1965. It was created in the sixteenth century by the Dutch navy and named after the Dutch word *pije*, which referred to its bullet-resistant wool melton cloth. It was short so as not to inhibit movement while climbing the rigging. It has become a classic from nerd preppy to stealth cool, having been reinterpreted by Alexander McQueen, Celine and Tom Ford.

The Breton top, worn by everyone from Chanel herself to Pablo Picasso, James Dean and Andy Warhol, is still a fashion staple. Its blue and white stripes – originally said to make it easier to spot someone who had fallen overboard – appeal to designers and consumers alike. Among its greatest fans is the *enfant terrible* of French fashion, Jean Paul Gaultier, who drew inspiration not only from the graphic qualities of navy blue and white but also from the long naval association with eroticism, with tight nautical-stripe T-shirts, sailor pants and tattoos to create an overtly sexual look.

In the 1960s, this look was transferred to the street via military surplus stores. Most recently, the 2016 resort collections from Karl Lagerfeld for Chanel, Thom Browne and Joseph Altuzarra featured nautical themes.

If a man in uniform is the symbol of masculine virility and sex appeal, the sailor with his lovers in every port has inspired some of the world's most tragic love stories, from Puccini's *Madam Butterfly* to Rainer Werner Fassbinder's more subversive homoerotic movie *Querelle* in 1982, which inspired Jean Paul Gaultier. From overt sex appeal to royal conservatism, the adaptability of nautical style continues to inspire fashion designers today.

Overleaf: US Coast Guards aboard the 'Eagle', London, 1957

Busnel, Spring/Summer 2013, Stockholm

Prada, Fall/Winter 2016–17, Milan

People's Liberation Army Navy soldiers at an arrival ceremony
for USS 'Fort McHenry', 1996

Mihara Yasuhiro, Spring/Summer 2015, Paris

Emre Erdemoglu, Spring/Summer 2015, Istanbul

London, 2012

Overleaf: US sailors, 1940

Paris, 2015

Sydney, 2015

Lanvin, Spring/Summer 2014, Paris

Ralph Lauren, Spring/Summer 2016, New York

The future King George V and his family aboard the HMS 'Crescent',
late 19th–early 20th century

New York, 2014

New York, 1942

Barcelona, 2015

'THE
GARMENTS
THAT BECOME
FASHIONABLE
MOST RAPIDLY AND

MOST COMPLETELY ARE THOSE

WHICH WERE ORIGINALLY
DESIGNED
FOR WARFARE,
DANGEROUS WORK,

OR STRENUOUS SPORT.'

—

ALISON LURIE, THE LANGUAGE OF CLOTHES

Tokyo, 2015

EAST MEETS WEST

Chinese silk, fiery dragons, Thai batik, Kashmiri pashminas: the distant lands of East Asia and India have fired the Western fashion imagination since Marco Polo went exploring. But fascination with Eastern and Indian uniform is far more recent, starting with the glamour of late nineteenth-century colonial troops in French Indochina (now Vietnam, Cambodia and Laos), continuing through the massed parades of the Chinese People's Liberation Army and the Soviet Red Army to the adoption of nonmilitary uniform that came with communist revolution throughout the region.

During the Cold War, the West viewed such clothing as alien, the uniform of the ideological 'enemy'. However, as shown by the huge success of the Metropolitan Museum of Art's blockbuster 2014 exhibition 'China: Through the Looking Glass', that attitude has changed. The West has embraced the East, or at least interpreted it in film costume and fashion through its very western filter. The Met exhibition presented clothes by Vivienne Tam, John Galliano for Dior and Vivienne Westwood inspired by Chinese dress, while Chinese-born Guo Pei merged Western style with the traditions of her homeland.

In addition to the more glamourous interpretations of Eastern costume, the uniformity and utilitarianism of China's communist clothing has also had a lasting appeal to Western designers and consumers. China's communist leader Mao Zedong understood that, while fashion divides, uniforms unite. If people dress alike, they are easier to persuade to think alike as signs of individuality are symbolically erased. Mao dressed the whole country in a shapeless version of military uniform that made no distinction for gender or rank. Although the palette included red and blue, the green uniforms of the army were seen as the most prestigious, the ambition of millions of Chinese children.

The Mao suit, or *Zhongshan* suit, was originally introduced to China in 1912 by Mao's later enemy, Chiang Kai-shek, as a combination of Western trousers and oriental tunic. After coming to power, Mao promoted a simplified, looser version of the suit for professionals and government leaders. The plain tunic has no distinctive features, but is said to be full of symbolism: its four pockets, five central buttons and three buttons on each cuff have various meanings attached to them, generally adhering to Chinese principles of balance and harmony.

The utilitarian impulse behind Chinese uniform inspired Yves Saint Laurent, who in 1971 used it for one of his early women's ready-to-wear collections. At the height of the Cold War, his references to Communism outraged his critics. But fashion answers to no one, least of all social conscience. Saint Laurent would further explore Asia in his tour de force Russian Opera and Chinese collections (in 1976 and 1977, respectively). Saint Laurent embraced the romance and decadence of the Silk Road, as seen in his wildly successful Opium fragrance campaign.

Today the utilitarian symbolism of Chinese clothing is echoed in the West by those who wear concisely edited clothing, as exemplified by some high-profile leaders and CEOs. Halston wore a signature black turtleneck. Steve Jobs did the same with the addition of jeans, while Mark Zuckerberg wears only grey T-shirts and grey hoodies. Albert Einstein purchased multiples of the same suit to avoid having to think about what to wear. Such an approach relegates fashion to something frivolous and superficial.

It also echoes the world of the superhero, who wears a utilitarian uniform in the quest for justice. Superheroes frequently echo 1940s and 1950s Soviet propaganda images, which could be inserted into any comic book, with their bold colours and their superhuman heroes. In 1989, the designer Thierry Mugler published a book of photographs in homage to communist propaganda, providing the perfect backdrop for his sharp-shouldered silhouettes and genetic harmony. Similar clothing was adopted by musicians of the Krautrock scene in 1960s Germany, which was more influenced by East German socialism and industrialization than hippie flower power, as seen in the utilitarian uniforms of later bands such as Kraftwerk or even Depeche Mode.

The Berlin Wall came down in 1989, ending the Cold War and since, China has opened its doors. This has led to the opening up of the fashion world too, for example, Guo Pei has designed spectacular clothes for Rihanna, and fashion collections in 2015 from Valentino, Just Cavalli and Alexander McQueen, to mention a few, included luxuriously tailored Chinese dragons, fiery red feathers and Mao collars. Thus the boundaries between utility and frivolity are shifting – and will continue to do so, because this is one of the great struggles at the heart of all fashion.

Overleaf and following spread: *Vogue*, China, April 2010

'THE

IMITATION

OF THE

MILITARY

UNIFORM

HAS TRIUMPHED OVER THE

ORIGINAL

PROTOTYPE.'

—

HOLLY BRUBACH, THE NEW YORK TIMES

North Korean soldier, 2008

Italy, 2014

Balmain, Fall/Winter 2014–15, Paris

Etro, Spring/Summer 2013, Milan

Beijing, 1990

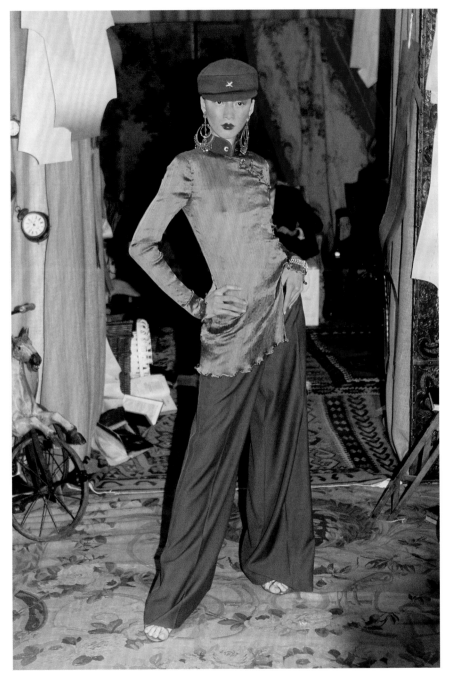

Christian Dior, Spring 1999, Paris

Overleaf: Soldiers at the Indian Army Camp, Great Pyramids, 1940

Etro, Spring/Summer 2013, Milan

Etro, Spring/Summer 2013, Milan

Yoshio Kubo, Spring/Summer 2016, Tokyo

Etro, Spring/Summer 2013, Milan

NOTORIOUS

For some, the appeal of military dress comes from its frank representation of power. Black leather coats, peaked officers' caps, jackboots, badges, straps and chains all give the wearer a latent menace or notoriety – and perhaps a hint of sexual deviance, thanks to their association not only with dominance but also with the decadent, androgynous world of Berlin in the years following World War I. In France, at the same time, Coco Chanel made her name by creating the androgynous 'La Garçonne' look, named for a 1922 novel by Victor Margueritte about the sexual adventures of a young woman with mannish bobbed hair and a penchant for men's clothing.

The clothes of military power carry suggestions of oppression, intimidation and brutality, with their echoes of the Nazi Brownshirts or Mussolini's fascist Blackshirts. In Nazi Germany, Hitler's secret police, the Gestapo, became associated with long, dark leather coats and peaked caps. In Hollywood movies, they often wore black uniforms, although in reality they more usually wore the grey field uniform of the equally-feared Schutzstaffel (SS), Hitler's elite protection forces. The sharp uniform was studded with badges of power – twin collar 'runes' or 'bolts' standing for SS, swastikas, gold shoulderboards, oak leaves indicating a general's rank, SS eagles and cuff bands.

In the early 1930s, the Nazis reintroduced the *totenkopf*, or death's head – a skull that had been braided onto the headwear of Prussian and German hussars from the eighteenth century to World War I. The new badge was adopted by the SS. For the victims of the SS, the skull's symbolism was one of intimidation. Today the death's head has been adopted by biker gangs such as the Hell's Angels – or even embroidered on preppy chino trousers with no reference to its sinister origin.

German Luftwaffe pilots wore black leather to keep them warm at high altitudes. After the war, similar jackets were taken up by American biker gangs, again to shield the wearer from bitter winds at high speeds. Marlon Brando wore one in the 1953 movie *The Wild One*, and Elvis Presley paired a high-collared leather jacket with black leather trousers in his famous 1968 televised comeback concert. In the 1970s, black leather was appropriated by gay subcultures and fetishists (Karl Lagerfeld designed fetish costumes for the art movie *Maîtresse* in 1976). David Bowie wore a black leather jacket on the cover of *Heroes* in 1977, while the punks led by Vivienne

Westwood adopted not only leather but also wholesale Nazi imagery in a subversive gesture intended to provoke outrage.

As leather and military elements spread through music and popular culture, their associations with decadence, androgyny, and film noir influenced the New Romantic movement that emerged in London in the early 1980s, centered on the weekly Blitz nightclub. Short of cash, the 'Blitz Kids' created weekly ensembles from thrift stores, drawing on a vast archive of military coats, jackets and military accoutrements, as well as Zoot suits with padded shoulders reminiscent of old Hollywood war movies. Their influence is evident in the costumes in the pivotal 1982 movie *Blade Runner* and in the way designer Antony Price dressed rock stars from Bryan Ferry to Duran Duran. Price dressed Blitz promoter and singer Steve Strange in a highly stylized black leather suit – fittingly photographed by the German–Australian photographer Helmut Newton, who was renowned for his sexually charged, black-and-white images. The double-breasted, asymmetrical jacket with Nehru collar – based on the Luftwaffe jacket – became a classic silhouette and a staple for designers from Giorgio Armani to Comme des Garçons, Ann Demeulemeester to Diesel.

S&M fetish fashion would evolve in the late 1980s and early 1990s, when Thierry Mugler and Gianni Versace brought leather, straps and studs to the fashion runway: 'S&M-Lite', as some of the fashion press dubbed it. But the more accessible and glamorous it seemed, its message became more complicated. More recently, the French house of Balmain studded hussar jackets with Swarovski crystal to create a rock-n-roll look that harked back to the decadence and excess of the 1980s, for which there is an ever-increasing nostalgia.

Such an approach may seem far removed from the sinister, impenetrable black leather clothes of the military, of tyrants, executioners and spies. But while memory, especially fashion memory, is highly selective, the message of black clothes remains the same. This is dress as both a threat and a form of defence. As World War II passes further into the past, the clothes' direct association with one of history's darkest periods might fade, but they continue to be symbols of defiance, decadence and deviancy.

Overleaf: *Interview*, November 2014

Gareth Pugh, Spring/Summer 2014, Paris

Gareth Pugh, Fall/Winter 2015, London

Ann Demeulemeester, Fall/Winter 2015, Paris

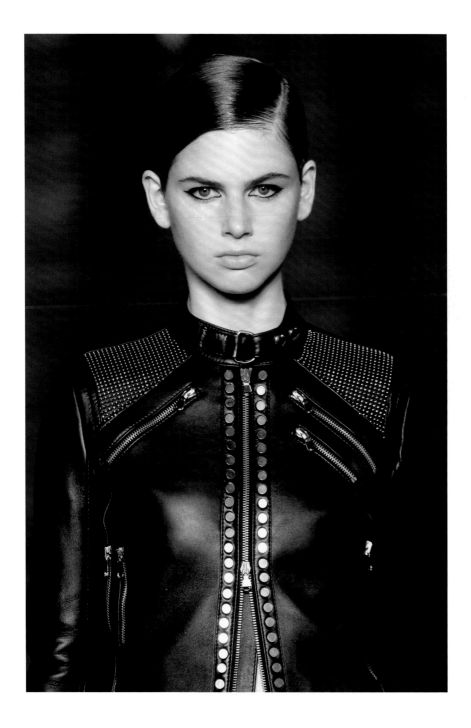

Diesel, Spring 2015, New York

The Swedish School Of Textiles, Spring/Summer 2013, Stockholm

Rudsak, 20th Anniversary Show, 2014, Toronto

Loewe, Fall/Winter 2011–12, Paris

London, 2012

'UNIFORMS,

ESPECIALLY MILITARY STYLES,

SYMBOLIZE AUTHORITY,

WHILE ALSO CARRYING AN

EROTIC EDGE.'

—

VALERIE STEELE

Jason Wu, Fall 2012, New York

Paris, 2015

Overleaf: *V Man*, September 2011

Balmain, Fall/Winter 2016–17, Paris

Ponystep, September 2012

Chicago, 2016

Sydney, 2014

Paris, 2012

Istanbul, 2014

'WE LIVE IN

VIOLENT TIMES,

AND THE

VIOLENT
TENOR OF LIFE

IS CLEARLY PRESENT

IN EVERYONE'S

SARTORIAL

CONSCIOUSNESS.'

—

ANNE HOLLANDER, SEX AND SUITS

Michael Kors, Fall 2013, New York

Thierry Mugler, Spring/Summer, 1997, Paris

Chloe, Fall/Winter 2011–12, Paris

1810
Bell-bottoms are introduced in the
US Navy to allow sailors greater
unencumbered movement

1846
Queen Victoria dresses her four-year-old
son Prince Albert Edward in a miniature
sailor suit

1857
Soldiers in the British Army adopt khaki
uniforms after the Indian Mutiny makes
it necessary to adapt uniform to the hot
climate and they become the official
uniform for the advance into Abyssinia
in 1867

1879
Thomas Burberry designs the trench coat
after inventing waterproof gabardine

1898
The US Navy issues white T-shirts for
sailors during the Spanish-American
War – inspired by nineteenth-century
undergarments

The US Army adopts khaki uniform

1912
The *Zhongshan*, or tunic suit, becomes
popular in China and later becomes
synonymous with Mao Zedong

1913
Coco Chanel begins to reference military
styles with sailor blouses for women,
followed by maritime striped jersey for
casual clothes

Drab colours become standard in military
uniform

1914
The trench coat, designed by Thomas
Burberry, becomes standard wear for
British officers in World War I

The French Camouflage Corps adopt
camouflage schemes designed by Lucien-
Victor Guirand de Scévola, André Mare
and others

1915
Uniforms become mass produced in
factories resulting in the disappearance
of detailing

1917
Inspired by the design of Renault tanks,
Louis Cartier creates the Cartier Tank
watch and presents the first prototype to
US General John Pershing

The strategy of dazzle camouflage is
employed by the British Navy

1919
Cartier releases the Tank watch and
it becomes a must-have, worn by
Jacqueline Kennedy and Andy Warhol
among others in the 1970s

1930
Khaki-coloured clothing becomes popular
as leisurewear in the United States

1931
The US Navy-designed A-2 becomes the
iconic flying jacket

1933
The *totenkopf* – or death head – is reintroduced by the Nazis as the SS badge

1937
Ray Ban creates 'Aviators', protective eyewear for the US Air Force

1939
Gary Cooper stars in the movie *Beau Geste*, bringing the legionnaire aesthetic to mainstream audiences

1940
Women carry versions of army shoulder bags because they allow more room for bandages, medicine, flashlights and other necessities during wartime

1941
Windbreakers – waist-length jackets with fitted waistlines adapted from British Royal Air Force jackets of the 1940s and made from nylon, wool or gabardine – become popular for men and boys

1942
Humphrey Bogart wears a trench coat as Rick Blaine in *Casablanca* and it achieves iconic status

1943
US General Dwight D. Eisenhower requests improvements on a waist-cropped British battle jacket – the Eisenhower-style jacket is still in circulation today

1953
From black leather boots and jackets to oversized goggles, the costumes in *The Wild One* starring Marlon Brando draw heavily on the notorious style of the Italian fascists and Nazis

1954
Marilyn Monroe wears a long-sleeve Army green uniform to visit US soldiers in Korea

1959
Fidel Castro liberates Cuba and popularizes army fatigues as daywear

1960
Designer Pauline Trigere debuts her pea coat and skirt ensemble in New York

Yves Saint Laurent, designing for Christian Dior, is called for compulsory army service in France after multiple deferments. He serves for twenty days but the experience prompts a nervous breakdown that leads to his dismissal at Dior

1961
Yves Saint Laurent opens his own fashion house and recreates the pea coat with deluxe fabrics and gold buttons

1964
The concert film *T.A.M.I Show* features Toni Basil as a go-go dancer wearing a pair of bell-bottoms. By 1967, bell-bottoms are *de rigueur* for hippies and by 1970 they become a key element of the uniform of anti-war protestors in the United States

1965
Paco Rabanne launches his shimmering minidresses made of linked plastic or

metal discs, inspired by knights' armour in the Middle Ages

Bob Dylan popularizes the pea coat by making it part of his signature look

1966
'I Was Lord Kitchener's Valet', a store specializing in vintage military clothing, opens on Portobello Road, London, with Eric Clapton, Mick Jagger and John Lennon as loyal customers

1967
The Beatles release the album 'Sgt. Pepper's Lonely Hearts Club Band' and wear brightly coloured hussar jackets as costumes

1968
Yves Saint Laurent introduces his Safari collection

1971
Jimi Hendrix buys a nineteenth-century hussar jacket and wears it to perform and protest against the Vietnam War

During the anti-war movement, Yves Saint Laurent causes uproar by showing camouflage on the runway

The ironic appropriation of Army-Surplus khakis, cargo pants continues apace

Camouflage-print bikinis, short-shorts and thongs become hippie-chic unisex must-haves in Saint Tropez, France

1981
The movie *Indiana Jones and the Raiders of the Lost Ark* is released starring Harrison Ford and causes US Army Air Corp-style aviator jackets to fly off the racks

1982
Rainer Werner Fassbender releases the homoerotic movie *Querelle*, which inspires Jean Paul Gaultier

1983
Celebrated art director Peter Saville designs the eye-catching cover for the Orchestral Manoeuvres in the Dark album 'Dazzle Ships' using a dazzle pattern

1985
Jean Paul Gaultier launches 'Le Male' a scent for men with the first of many subsequent advertising campaigns celebrating sailors sporting maritime stripes

1987
Stephen Sprouse obtains permission to use Andy Warhol's 'Camouflage' silkscreens for fabric for his Fall 1987 and Spring 1988 collections

Michael Jackson begins his BAD world tour, wearing military jackets on stage

1991
Ralph Lauren Spring women's collection includes military inspired designs: 'Being tough, being strong, being a warrior', says Lauren, who served in the US Army from 1962 to 1964

1994
Prada's military-influenced collection
is dubbed 'utility chic'; Miuccia Prada
calls uniforms 'the most reassuring and
elegant dictatorship'

Donatella Versace designs satin combat
trousers at Versace

1997
Panerai Italian military submarine watch
manufacturer is purchased by Richemont
and re-envisioned as a luxury brand

1998
The Gap's 'Khaki Swing' ad campaign
proves that chinos and military-style
trousers are officially mainstream

2000
Jean Paul Gaultier's Spring Summer
Couture collection includes a voluminous
ball gown made of densely packed tulle
in a jungle camouflage print, which the
actress Sarah Jessica Parker wears to an
awards ceremony in the US

2001
John Galliano designs a silk camouflage
evening dress for Christian Dior

2006
The M-65 field jacket worn by Robert De
Niro in the film Taxi Driver inspires Junya
Watanabe's Spring men's collections

2008
Marc Jacobs and the artist Takashi
Murakami collaborate to create
camouflage monogram for Louis Vuitton

2010
Balmain's Spring collection salutes army
fatigues

Christopher Bailey redesigns the aviator
jacket for Burberry

2012
Simon Spurr applies dazzle pattern to
the runway, crediting his inspiration to
Normal Wilkinson

2013
From Marc Jacobs to Givenchy,
camouflage patterns rule the runways

2014
'China: Through the Looking Glass'
exhibition is presented at the
Metropolitan Museum of Art, New york

2015
Marc Jacobs' Spring collection includes
army-style jackets inspired by the jackets
worn by Grace Slick of the band Jefferson
Airplane in the 1960s as an antiwar
statement

Versace's collection is an homage to
camouflage to make women stand
out - reversing the purpose for which
camouflage was originally intended

2016
For the Tommy Hilfiger Fall collection, the
fashion show set is built to resemble a
steam liner, and supermodel Gigi Hadid
wears a gold sequined sailor dress

Acknowledgements

This book is dedicated to the memory of my father David Eric Godbold.

Words cannot express my gratitude to my editor William Norwich for his professional advice and assistance. I owe special thanks to Colin McDowell for his introduction and I would also like to thank all those at Phaidon who contributed to the creation of this book, particularly Rosie Pickles, Tim Cooke, Ellen Christie, Aaron Garza, Emmanuelle Peri and Jenny Faithfull. This book would not have been possible without the support and encouragement from Ann Frank, Christopher and Karin Ross, Patrice Farameh, Kevin Menard, Margo West, Nick Rhodes, Christopher Wold, Diana and Paul Frank, Stephen Kenn, Nan Dillon, Tony Glenville, Natasha Esch, Carl Davis, Margo West, Anthony and Karin Godbold and my mum Patricia Hoffman.

Akg-images: IAM 126; Bridgeman Images: National Army Museum, London 20; Camera Press 45, 51, 125, 178, 179, 180, 184, Camera Press: Andrea Simms 53; Corbis: ©Condé Nast Archive 165, ©Jean Jacques Ceccarini/epa 97, ©Marineau Elhage/epa 25, ©Jeremy Horner 18-19, ©Alain Keler/Sygma 90-91, ©Ki Price 24, ©Pierre Vauthey/Sygma 114; Juan Aldabaldetrecu/folio-id.com 85, Nikol Bartzoka folio-id.com 116-117; Getty Images: Brian Ach 75, Afro American Newspapers/Gado 44, Forrest Anderson 136, C. Balossini 28-29, Alessio Botticelli 71, Vanni Bassetti 50, 62, 109, 189, Miquel Benitez 149, Richard Bord 137, Margaret Bourke-White 166-167, Fernanda Calfat 110, 188, Vittorio Zunino Celotto 93, China Foto Press 107, Stefania D'Alessandro 163, 168, 171, Pietro D'Aprano 12, 58cl, 59cl, 59cr, 59fr, Antonio de Moraes Barros Filho 46, 59fl, 86, 92, 119, 127, 144, 201, Peter Michael Dills 89, 99, 123, Alfred Eisenstaedt 148, Timur Emek 147, 197, Frazer Harrison 199, Ian Gavan 72, Tim Graham 164, Koji Hirano 170, Hulton Archive, 10, IWM 104-105, Edward James 121, 183, Melodie Jeng 66, 67, 76, Keystone-France 82-83, Eric Lafforgue 160, Pascal Le Segretain 22, 106, 162, Magnus & Mads/Figarophoto/Contour Style 113, Danny Martindale 64, Caroline McCredie 118, 143, 195, Damien Meyer 77, Carl Mydans 140-141, Oleg Nikishin 124, George Pimentel 56, The Print Collector 11, 146, Ben A Pruchnie 138, Tulio M Puglia 94, 96, PYMCA 185, Andreas Rentz 134, 182, Kirstin Sinclair 31, 63, 74, 139, 142, 196, Robert Spangle 26, Kristy Sparow 120, Matthew Sperzel 55, 69, 194, Stocktrek Images 52, TPG 57, 151, ullstein bild 36, Universal History Archive 9, 115, William Vanderson 132-133, Pierre Verdy 200, Christian Vierig 47, 54, Victor Virgile 23, 49, 58fl, 58cr, 58fr, 60, 84, 87, 98, 135, 145, 169, Mark Von Holden 111, Slaven Vlasic 65, Peter White 21, 32, 192, Georgie Wileman 68, 70, JP Yim 181, Daniel Zuchnik 37, 108; Cameron McNee: Photo.: Cameron McNee/Stylist: Kenny Ho/Model: Sam Webb 30, Photo: Cameron McNee/Stylist: Crystal McClory/Model: Freddie Dresner & Supa Model Management 73; Quentin Shih: 156-157, 159; Kai Z Feng/trunkarchive.com 87, 190-191, Melanie Galea/trunkarchive.com 161, Gregory Harris/trunkarchive.com 176-177, Bjarne Jonasson/trunkarchive.com 35, Sebastian Mader/trunkarchive.com 193, Josh Olins/trunkarchive.com 33, Lee Oliveira/trunkarchive.com 27, Emma Summerton/trunkarchive.com 42–43.

Phaidon Press Limited
Regent's Wharf
All Saints Street
London N1 9PA

Phaidon Press Inc.
65 Bleecker Street
New York, NY 10012

phaidon.com

First published 2016
© 2016 Phaidon Press Limited

ISBN 978 0 7148 7246 9

A CIP catalogue record for this book is available from
the British Library and the Library of Congress.

Commissioning Editor: William Norwich
Project Editor: Rosie Pickles
Production Controllers: Sue Medlicott and Nerissa Vales
Design: Aaron Garza

Printed in China